n*e*

Listening, listening

This is Bob Cooper's third full collection of poems after a five-decade career which has also seen the publication of six pamphlets, some of which have been award-winning. True to form these latest poems deal with ordinary people, a number of whom, in a newly developed theme, have surreal encounters with historical literary figures. Bob's poems are ironic, funny and poignant with much underlying comment on our times.

If poetry is about voice it is also about listening. Bob writes what he hears in his unique and distinctive style.

To Duayne, Monika,
Alesha, Ruby,
Abigail and Dave,
with Love

Bob Cooper

Christmas '23

About Bob Cooper's poetry

...a humane and distinctive voice ... Bob Cooper is one of our most individual and impressive poets. He deserves to be widely read.
Peter Bennet

Poems that sparkle with humour and seduce with sadness.
Tim Allen

Always perfectly crafted, this is real poetry. Cooper illuminates lives with astounding compassion.
Angela Readman

Bob Cooper writes earthy poetry with a lyricist's touch.
Michael Bangerter

His particular eye brilliantly gives us the complexity of 'ordinary' lives.
Michael Standen

A writer who calls a spade a spade and knows how to dig with it...
Maura Dooley

I love their earthiness, little sinister bits, and all the wisdom, which is not shouted out loud, but thoughtfully hidden in or between the words and lines.
Taru Vuontisjärvi

About 'Listening, listening'

Bob Cooper's new collection is set in the contemporary moment, post-Brexit, labouring under the burdens of austerity, eyeing our callous and self-serving, self-styled 'betters', neatly reimagined here in the figure of 'Boris Falstaff'. Like Armitage, Cooper has a compassionate eye for our behaviours under pressure, and these poems are full of encounters and bearings of witness, statements of a nation in distress and seeking a supportive ear.

Bill Herbert.
Professor of Poetry & Creative Writing at Newcastle University

Bob Cooper with 'Listening, listening' turns the ordinary world into an extraordinary book. He has a deep power of observation and writes more than just poems. What is captivating is that as well as being wonderfully word-worthy each poem tells a close-your-eyes and run-the-poem through-your-mind story.

John Gorman
The Scaffold, Tiswas

Also by Bob Cooper

Poetry Collections

All We Know Is All We See (Arrowhead 2002)
Everyone Turns (Pindrop 2017)

Poetry Pamphlets

Bruised Echoes (Outposts 1977)
Light From The Upper Left (Smith Doorstop 1994)
Beyond Liathach (Tears In The Fence 1995)
Drinking Up Time (Redbeck Press 1997)
Pinocchio's Long Neb (Smith Doorstop 2000)
The Ideal Overcoat (Ward Wood 2012)

LISTENING, LISTENING

Bob Cooper

Naked Eye Publishing

Naked Eye Publishing

© Bob Cooper 2023

Book design and typesetting by Naked Eye

Cover illustration: Eddy Aigbe

ISBN: 9781910981290

www.nakedeyepublishing.co.uk

Acknowledgements

Versions of some of these poems have been published in the following magazines: Nine Muses, '14', Allegro, Atrium, Cake, Cannon's Mouth, Die DePfeffelschrift, Dreamcatcher, Dreich, Fire, Glove, The High Window, The Honest Ulsterman, Ink Sweat And Tears, London Grip, The Lake, The Ofi Press, Orbis, Poetry Scotland, Poetry Salzburg Review, The Rialto, Scratch, Snakeskin, Stand, The Waxed Lemon.

Versions of some of these poems have also appeared in the following anthologies: A Scream Of Many Colours (poetryspace 2019), Journeys (The Novels Project, The Poetry Kit 2020), Summer Anywhere (Dreich 2021), The Twelve Days Of Christmas (Ink Sweat & Tears 2021).

Two poems were prize-winners in respectively an Open University poetry competition and the Barnett Poetry Competition. One poem is from the prize-winning pamphlet Drinking Up Time (Redbeck Press 1997), and a revised version of another poem is from the Lumen Cold Weather Shelter Poetry prize-winning pamphlet The Ideal Overcoat (Ward Wood 2012). A series of poems stems from two poems in the Poetry Business prize-winning pamphlet Pinocchio's Long Neb (Smith Doorstop 2000).

For Helen

LISTENING, LISTENING

Speaking is listening to the language which we speak.

Martin Heidegger

…we were told that poetry is about voice, about finding a voice and speaking with this voice, but the older I get I think it's not about voice, it's about listening and the art of listening, listening with attention. I don't just mean with the ear; bringing the quality of attention to the world.

Kathleen Jamie

You can't fake listening. It shows.

Raquel Welch

Contents

Before sunrise, eating muesli, I decide that

today on the 7.24 from Moreton to Liverpool Central
I won't window-stare but really listen to him
who gets on each day at Leasowe, whose breathing's as loud
as everything he says, whose laugh, then cough, is as growl-heavy
as the broad zip on the scuffed black Adidas bag
he opens on his lap, rummaging for his flask of tea
where each cup's so strong we'll all smell it,
and a bacon sarnie double-wrapped in silver foil,
crinkled, from a Tupperware box with the loudest of lids

before pulling out a freezer bag of golf balls and walking round:
  top brands
he'll say with chewed-up comments about them landing in his
  back-garden –
five for a quid. Then he'll sit back down, sigh, sip from his mug

but I won't let him do that.
                    No,
                        before he gets up I'll ask
about things we may share: the smell of sleeping children,
an understanding of how cats' tails say what their mouths can't
and how we rarely hear sounds that can fill us with wonder
like when we hear an oboe, or brass cogs' quiet clicks in a clock

and how, at night, many miles apart, we each stand
at some open back door with the empty sea breeze
slipping through the fence, and gaze at nothing but
clouds as they hurry overhead, then large shapes
half-seeable in the darkness that seem, like us, to belong.

Abdulatif, now head of the family, says what matters

We've been promised windows with curtains,
beds, cupboards not shelves, a TV and fridge.
I have explained to my mother
how English does not always say
what it means, so saucepans
are for vegetables not just sauces
and teabag doesn't mean bag of tea.
In a while we will get used to British bread.

These are the last minutes of our journey,
two years from Syria, so much money,
and now the drive in a mini-bus to a flat
in Wallasey, the Wirral, England.

May my father, who became part of the sea
just when we'd sighted Europe – its lights
beyond the high waves – as the boat sank,
bless us and help me. My sister,
one year older than I, must now
wear a dark dress, a burka.
I don't like how men look at her.
My young brother is now eight and still quiet
yet patient and clever with his hands.
He will be an engineer to honour our father.
I will learn good English and Latin,
be a doctor like my dead uncle.
Soon we will have more documents.
I will find schools.

The minibus stops. I wake us all.
We see light beyond an opened door
as three women step forward to greet us.

To be continued

Right in front of where I sit on the bus the nonsense-sounds mum
pulls faces, coos to her wriggling child in a pram who reacts
with the full-on face thrill only all the world's babies know

as we tremble, jolt, sway in unison through sunlight
that flecks over us as we pass roadside winter trees,
the light resonant and deep, like in Clint Eastwood films
where he insisted scenes be shot in low-sun cloud-free skies.

Her orange coat with its faded stitching glows, the pram is scuffed,
its handle's blue plastic sleeve torn, bound round with masking tape,
but her white earrings are huge – how they jiggle – and her hair,
tightly combed, black, tied with a multi-coloured top-knot ribbon,
curls, semi-circles down, sways in front of her lowered brow
as she strokes the child's stained onesie, its hat too big for its head;
as his or her hands wiggle, grasp hers before generous, shrill squeals.

Then she stands, grips the handle, her foot releasing the brake;
manœuvres, pushes the pram and her child down the aisle. I love
how she bends, repeats *Yes, we'll soon see Grandma and Grandpa*

and how the child, now silent, looks up at the faces they pass
and I want to remember this, all of this, because it happened.

I go to the newsagents when I could get a whole box of pens online

because I want to exchange nods, greet others who are waiting
                                                      for the bus,
chat to the newsagent about the gale rattling his door as I pay
                                                      for a pen
before pausing, as I always do, to read the small ads pinned up
                                                  on his board:
Woodchurch Girls blazer and skirt age 11-12, shoes size 5,
                                                      all unworn

then walk to the corner where I see the sea at high tide,
                                                  feel the wind
as I stand there after it's passed across chilled nothingness,
                                                  and see
what no-one else sees: how it touches all that matters – makes
                                              a gull swerve,
makes waves spray onto the pavements and windows and doors
                                              behind me

and I feel as if there's a child who has paused because I've paused,
                                              who asks
what are you staring at? and I say n*othing,* which means everything
then, while knowing the touch of her hand in mine, she empties away,
                                              is gone
before I turn for home, the new pen in my breast pocket already warm.

Talking with an elderly Afghan asylum seeker at the bus-stop about Jorge Luis Borges

begins with him pointing at the book in my pocket,
So, do you say well about Borges?
I say, don't know, I've just bought it
so haven't yet read what he thinks about
anything. And he grins, says, *he died in exile,*
a Christian Argentinian. I'm Muslim

then he slowly speaks the title, *Labyrinth...*
So, please, what does that word mean for Borges?
Again I shrug, say, *no idea* (pause) *yet.*
I know he could speak (he goes on) *in Anglo Saxon -*
I will learn maybe after learn to speak modern English well,
then speak loud like him, The Dream Of The Rood.
I nod. He nods. We pause. We smile

and even though Borges is buried in Geneva he's not
beyond standing himself alongside each of us now,
where he tries to recall what's inside his book's covers
just like all writers have to when they get as old
as that black and white photo on the back flap.

I fumble for my bus pass, say, *good to meet you*
then, once on board, take the book from my pocket and read,
while Borges leans forward from the seat behind
but stands, also, next to the man at the bus stop
where they are both waving, and I and my Borges wave back,
and on turning the first page I find he's there too,
and in silence, that is where I begin.

On the Wallasey Bus with Paul Theroux's new lover

She points across me out of the bus window – *look,*
my local library – shut! I see graffitied doors.
Books, she says, I've always borrowed them. Loved them.
Their covers beneath thick scratched polythene, their pictures.
They became friends; some really difficult to return,
before I began doing what I do now. Sitting here all excited
till I get the kettle on then flit through its pages, impatient,
then settle with teapot and packet of biscuits, and begin.

I glance down at the bag on her lap; inside, an oblong shape.
She strokes it. *Sometimes in my head I say to a chapter,*
I love how you describe things – tell me again.
My bedside table is home to the world, and to people
that soon become friends. They soothe me to sleep
while I stand with the curious, walk marble floors in palaces,
eat foods I could never describe, have mysteries explained,
feel astonishments, fall deeply in love, cry then smile.

She stares at me, grins – *see my bus pass, library card?*
My passport and visas to circle the globe! And this is my stop.
Today, Paul Theroux will thrill me in exciting places. Soon
I'll be sipping while sharing a journey better than this. Cheerio.

When Virgil met Dante

A boulevard (I say to Dante while we snaffle Pane Toscanos)
originally was a bulwark where Dutch people walked and talked
as they gazed at those below them from their city walls,
but now everyone's on our level. And he interrupts – so
(because he's good with questions, while spluttering crust flakes
like a tree dropping leaves in autumn) – did they talk in circles
like us, sat here people-watching but pretending not to stare?

Beyond our bench, circle-dancers circle; Florentine buskers play,
harmonising Beatles songs, each sung about a special girl.
We listen, recall George Harrison in A Hard Day's Night
saying in a scouse accent, *grotty* – more beautiful than grotesque,
whilst nothing like a grotto where more loving words get said.

Have you ever loved? he asks, eyes sad as Robin Hood's
when he gazed after the (just-invented) beauty Maid Marion
(in the new version of a story he'd only just half-read where
they'd been starved of affection). Don't abandon hope, I say.
Everyone's in love, and not only with lovers who can show us
everything that matters. We all have dreams we can't control –
dreams such as loving others like we should love ourselves
and I pause because he's chewing things over, then I continue,
This straat should be called Viale Il Canto because there's seats
beneath trees where people who sit longer than buskers' lyrics
will hear simple mysteries in the language of birds – I'm here.
I hear you, too. Is there danger? Is there food? Is it time to mate?

So now he's silent, perhaps looking to scatter crumbs
for a peahen or sparrows … when Beatrice on a mountain bike
does a wheelie straight past us, straight-armed, staring ahead,
loudly singing a song with alternate Italian lines then Dutch;
when above everyone's head height as she power-pedals past
through the ariel circling wheel we see horrified faces watch.

One of the times when Willie Long-Legs and Laudanum
Sam met Mazy Mary and Sarah Snuggles

Willie Long Legs one-hands the wheel, twirls the radio dial
                    till it plays fiddle tunes.
Laudanum Sam then lolls his head back while, full volume,
                    they sing, extemporising harmonies,
to Robbie Burns' love-lorn then love-rejoicing choruses and lyrics
                    before Sam asks at Penrith
Right to go home? Or left to the Hall on Sockburn Lane
                    hours away through each twisting bend?

They turn left. Cruise up past Stanmore's summit cafe,
                    see in the night sky
a red blossom. Teesside's Iron Smelting Furnaces. *The world,*
                    says Willie, *like us is on the cusp of change.*
They speed through Hurworth where young Brontes didn't sleep
                    instead wrote stories in notebooks,
Because, Sam says, *we and they are high-revving utter Romantics*
                    driving full tilt toward what's yet to get writ.

Tyres squeal as, like the silent slow river, they turn at Neasham
                    where Peg Powler once rose from reeds
sang beyond black waters to lure her victims to silence
                    and the Sockburn Worm prowled
until chopped to myth by a falchion; where, now, a child wakes
                    when headlights slice light across curtains
as they roar past. Then he lies wide-eyed remembering,
                    colourful as a dream, his school painting –
a bright ship, a big bird, the wide ocean –
                    sees it again drawing-pinned to the wall
before he begins to pillow-whisper lines about daffodils
                    that dance along verges
on his school-day walk to the village – while their exhaust's rasp
                    makes racehorses open wide eyes,

24

no longer twitch legs in their hurdler's dreams, as the car's beams
        light up tree-boles
which gleam like shanks each side of the road while branches
        stretch overhead
like splayed manes, frozen in a sport page's photograph

before the car skids over grass at the edge of the final bend;
        before they stare
between hedgerows, accelerate up the final steepness
        for a first glimpse, rising up
to where stars glitter, but below and far brighter is the glow
        from two upstairs lit windows
where, with knees tucked up, shawls snug among pillows,
        memorised poems are whispered
from identical books, one inscribed *All my love, Willie,*
        the other *All my love, Sam,*
as gravel's thrown high, hits the window as faces stare up.
        Then faces stare down.
A long pause. The lock's slow turn. Hushed moments. Hugs
        like understated pressure on blank paper
when poems are being written on their other sides
        where words follow astonished words.

The Famous Five go on holiday

*Or when Messrs Wordsworth, Keats, Constable, Turner, and Miss
Bronte rented a holiday cottage in Neston*

It was almost five in the morning, not yet dawn,
when, one by one, they appeared in the kitchen.
No-one spoke, they stood there, smiled, watched
Willie Long-Legs bend over the bread board,
slide slices into the toaster. When they sprang up
Little-Johnny K pulled them out, scraped on butter
then quieter smears of strawberry jam.
Hot Eyes Emily picked one up, took a bite

broke the silence

mentioned the way heads sink into soft pillows
then Tall-Cloud John spoke of flannelette pyjamas' softness
and Light-Headed Turner of cool sheets on leg-stretched feet,
but no-one asked why they'd woken just as daylight
began to reveal the cottage they'd rented for the week

because the clock

whirred then chimed as Willie Long-Legs tugged a cord,
venetian blinds squeaked, quick-clattered open;
as fingers held toast and they stared into the light

before Hot-Eyes Emily

stood at the door, turned the key, tugged it open.
Fresh air and birdsong rushed in, hovered,
touched them, silenced them, blessed them
before she ushered them out to greet more of it

breathe it in

where they faced a simple yet surreal sunrise,
one that must happen here every cloudless day.
They took out their phones, ignored each other,
dropped toast – the birds would love that –
took images, jam-fingered unpredicted phrases
then posted them as they stared at its brightening light
that would get shared, re-shared, again, again.

*Mr Yeats's radio recording of when he and Mr Pound spent
a February afternoon in Hoylake*

*(Oh, and could you please play Rod Stewart's Sailing after I've
finished and before I read the poem? It was on when we were in the
Co-op. That's what started me off. Thanks)*

I'd tried not to listen as Ezra passed freezers
        of fish, flesh, and fowl
while chuntering on about poems looking like polystyrene trays
        needing to be thawed,
their cellophane cut, then cooked, nibbled at. Instead
        make them fresh, new!

he said in his loud American accent as if commanding
        their frozenness to change.
I looked away – at sausages: Lincolnshire, Cumberland and,
        more costly, Oxford
then he stared too – *British poems are like these links, just
        slightly different shades –*

and leant forward, prodded them. I guessed I'd hear, *Each has
        rows of neat stanzas ...*
but instead he said, *Let's have the Oxfords, they include more
        intriguing things,*
before he threw back his head as if performing, shouted,
        Boloney, polony,

is what I ate as a child in Jenkintown. But I'd heard it all before,
        the great
and the grot. So I interrupted, asked a question, *What rhymes with
        orange?*
and his quick wit replied: *A sausage maker's syringe that
        squeezes meat into skins!*

Later, outside our camper van, as a gale blew in from the Irish Sea,
       I heard him
bellow into the overwhelming spray an almost finished canto,
       while I sat, wrote,
sliced bread, pricked sausage-skins, heard them sizzle, beckoned
       him to come in

to chomp his sandwich which was held in mid-air, his full mouth
       wide open,
while I read about Byzantium as our cramped van-home trembled
       as if sailing
to a horizon-place words might reveal, yet our Satnav
       would never show.

Rilke in his Audi on the M53

His car radiator looks like a snarl
and sun on the windscreen hides a face,
while where it's travelled from, where it's going,
only the one no-one sees knows. All I know
is its paintwork's panther-black gleam
and two headlights that glare in my mirror.
In reverse I read the number plate: R1LKE,
see it – like an ear twitching – indicate,
then hear what's no longer a purr
but the power of movement, a roar.

Boswell and Johnson's unremarkable day-trip

We boarded at Ullapool,
sat inside because we knew
it would be windy. It was.

At Stromness we sat in a coach,
walked, too-quick – then – too – slow,
heads down round a stone circle,
along a spray flecked row of thatched cottages
to a broch whose walls sheltered us,
then back to the Tesco car park
for an ice cream before our return.

Johnson was whiskyless, silent.
Sometimes someone opened a door
and the wind blew in. But mostly
in the ferry's slow sways, thick glass,
thicker than the coach,
kept everything out.

With Alyia on her first New Year's Day walk

which begins with blowing on hands while we cross fields
before we each touch lichen smears on a damp gate,
hear its creak, the latch's clatter as it closes

then stride a hard path up, up, up onto the moor,
see lifeless cotton grass, heather, quiver in the wind
to reach the stone circle's boulders too cold to sit on

which is where we wish to be, as we pause,
eat samosas with gloved hands as a standing lunch;
as we walk round, look at every curving horizon

then up to slow, thin clouds, the sun's low zenith,
and down to where brightness and dullness alter colours
before, shivering, we turn, face the wind's silence,

quickly stroll a different route of bare-earth fields
where unseen wheat seeds already swell.

Summer's evening, winter's afternoon, and night's sunlit darkness

In July on top of the last climb of the day, cows filed past.
They couldn't know beauty, though with udders bulged
slow necks swayed, eyes saw the world only cows see
as they walked through it while we coiled our rope, gazed
way beyond them, their field, over acres of trees to the sun
that paused, while birds boisterously sang, one against another,
before it touched the horizon, slid late-evening suddenly down.

Then in November when everything, yet nothing, was different,
cows still processed below, but only crows cawed from harsh trees
whose colours were shredded, carried by a keen wind that blew
into, through, layered sweaters as hands were shoved into armpits
to find warmth enough to untie rope-knots before clambering down
as the huge dull-red sun that had thrown its glow onto all but shadows
left our world while carabiners chinked into packs. Jackets were zipped,
the walk to the car began, the cold forgotten as breath rose with small talk

and there was still beauty – frizzled leaves whisked across the bonnet,
one gusted to the dashboard, frail-veined, dry, as it held enough light
to defy darkness – and all is now curled leaf-like under a duvet
in night-time hours when remembering as arthritic climbers do.

Those on the ball before darkness surrounds them

Leaves twirl down where four boys and five girls
holler each other's names as they pass, dribble
on grass that's held wetness all day. They give-and-go,
shoot between goalpost jackets.

One dives, saves,
others make Cruyff turns, show stepover skills,
and everything beyond all this is also here
in this November afternoon as they kick, run, tackle,
yell, *next goal's the last, okay?*

then celebrate it,
peel leaves off the ball, shake water off coats,
see gloom has surrounded all but their game,
then, with we've-all-won-it-all light in their eyes,
they stand below clouds of luminous breath.

Those who share the earth
for David and Abigail Gava and family

Side by side they plant carrots, talk Shona
with the guy pulling up weeds on the next allotment
as they stoop, spread seeds thinly, press lightly down

on local soil near where chomolia gleams in the sun,
shelters pumpkins already growing fat.
In July's heat Matabeleland's winter is as far away

as their shared language and knowledge are close.
They stand, stretch, glance back at the maize
only three-quarters the height they recalled that it grew

then lower their heads, continue. Each heel-shuffle
inches them further north till legs touch the barrow
wheeled from their semi-detached home.

Since all of you eat what's
grown I hope you also plant
what's grown. So this poem is
not(d) not just for Mum and
Dad!

What garden centre staff whisper loudly to each other before they open

Where passengers on flights see lavender and rape fields,
strawberry crops have no pickers singing songs from Romania,
refugees return home their carrier bags full of apples and plums,
    let us call on the Green Man.

Where spiders feast nightly on aphids in greenhouses' moist air,
bees laden with pollen silently nuzzle between petals,
park-keepers unlock gates, hear a thrush sing louder than traffic,
    let us call on the Green Man.

Where Keep Out signs fall, get overgrown by weeds, rot,
roadside's grass is uncut because of council cut-backs,
acorns are planted by residents outside care homes
    let us call on the Green Man.

Where mums and toddlers concentrate, make daisy chains,
a picnic blanket is laid for a cliff-top lingering lunch,
lovers walk through woodland's scent of wild garlic
    let us call on the Green Man.

Where Friends Of The Lake District plant daffodil bulbs
                              in the rain,
Little Gidding's hedgerows are a blizzard of May blossom,
A Midsummer Night's Dream's played out in council estates
    let us call on the Green Man.

Where hosepipes forks and rakes carried from allotment sheds,
workers like us fill shelves with seed packets, spray plants in tubs,
and there's breath-like mist on windows where shrubs blossom
    then the Green Man has heard, has been.

As it lightly cradles a whole pale moon,
raising it above rooves, the crescent moon rises

late on a suburban Upton midnight

while wives turn a page, muffle yawns,
how many men are now standing in socks

bare-legged as they thread trousers through a hanger
then close the wardrobe door, peep between curtains

and see its fresh curve lift astonishing darkness
as when witnessed in childhood – an ungiven gift

still in clear focus above light's hazy pollution,
the mute slowness of a new moon?

And soon they will lie with the light of their thoughts,
neither realising all they ever wanted is here

as it is when no-one looks up, no-one wonders,
as it is in the silence of their dark bedroom right now.

A retired shipyard draughtsman hears the ghost-pilot's song

He stands, blueprints now memories, grips the rail tightly, sees
the current's strength that forces brown water, as mist solidifies,

drifts downstream to become self-fulfilling shapes of ships
longer than warehouses, masts tall as cranes at Cammell Laird's

then hears a ghost-pilot sing as they pass the floodlit Three Graces
mentioning trade routes, merchandise, vessels' names, their owners

while the moon's light gleams on their stones and long-dark windows,
shimmers on the river, reaches him. Watery-eyed he turns, walks

having heard on the breeze in the Mersey's not-yet-dawn flow
laments that float over its surface. He sings their echoes.

Pensioners waiting for the night-bus quietly sing 'In The Midnight Hour'

because they remember being teenagers, as lively together
as those they see hollering choruses as they cross the street

neat-stepping as they sashayed, arms wide, full-volume lyrics
                                        from the soul of songs
knowing as little as those who yell wide-mouthed melodies now

declaring the tunefulness of loving, a kiss's meaning,
                                        oh so close cuddling,
as well as the dark lines of bright tears, inconsolable rejections

as they shimmied head-lowered bodies in dimly-lit dance halls.
So, now, stood relaxed with sweat-drying clubbers at the bus-stop

they'll return home as their clock chimes, to tap spoons
                                        on Ovaltine mug rims
and again softly Pickett-duet sing as they slowly sway upstairs.

What the district nurse never included in her report

How his smile muscles were so under-used that
when they twisted, tightened, I was always surprised

or how he'd let slip the holiday he'd chosen unexpectedly
never happened, as, after closing his suitcase –
his coat buttoned up – he'd made a mug of tea, sat down,
had a sip, then another and ignored the taxi's beeping horn

or how his motionless dog seemed nervous of me,
and he talked of its medications more than his own,
and blinked, the dog blinking too as they watched each other,
and it would relax with a sigh when I stood up to go.

Or how with faltering eye-contact he'd close the door:
I rarely open this now. It's cold where you are.

Two room-visits in a twelve-hour shift

I help her stand, look out the window.
From the fourth floor we see so much:
sky, church spires, the road beyond trees.
Strong hands, Andréa, like my daughter.
Despite my name-badge she calls me that
as if I'm a care worker she knew
who worked here when she arrived.
See how I've come up in the world, she says
each time we stare down on autumn,
its sunlit colours, bright patterns
that belong to us both from elsewhere;
that match her loose-fitting blouse.

I lower her back to her chair
then we repeat what we said yesterday,
Have you taken your pills?
What pills? she says.
Your pills, I repeat,
looking at the row of three
on a saucer with the half-full teacup
she'll sip from as she swallows them
before I take the tray away.

In the afternoon I knock gently,
reclose the door quietly, hear soft snores
before I stroke her hand to wake her, lift her.
Strong hands... we stand at the window.
See how I've come up in the world
she repeats while we stare down,
then when I've adjusted the cushions
I help her sit. She frowns, *my pills.*
Where are my pills? I smile, say,
Maybe you took them after breakfast?
Ah, yes, Andréa, maybe I did.

*Mrs. Ryle buys a photograph album from the British Heart
Foundation shop*

with its pages, empty polythene sleeves
soon to be filled from the life she's lived.
She'll seal in the living, the dead,
where, when its opened, they'll look up at her,
smile, and she'll smile back.

Yet now, she feels it's hiding ghosts.

When she turns pages their faint rustles
are loud whispers calling out names
she'll never hear, and on the shelf,
when she sees only its spine, tales are told
only the back of her photos will know.

Ob-La-Di, Ob-La-Da

She rubs lipstick from teeth, washes hands,
straightens her brooch, glances at her hair,
brushes it again, walks downstairs
                            slowly
checks her bag: purse, bus-pass, phone,
then, stood by the door, puts on her new scarf,
zips up her coat, blows her nose,
                            leaves.
Eyes watery when she sees herself
in the bus shelter's glass. Hair ruffled,
hands cold.
           Today is a fine day to die

but then she surprises herself –
                       starts to sing –
no mournful dirge, but a song of joy.

Life is cruel to softly remind her of pleasures
when she has to wait, stood in a queue like this!
But she trills on, and as the words spill out
she's surprised
                because texting while stood on the bridge
then hitting 'send', then stepping off into thin air
is not for today.
              Remaining still, her melody loud
she lets the bus pass,
                  trips, light-footed, back home.

Change and no change

It's raining. I'm in the bus shelter, chilled and wet.
They're at the phone box. She's inside, talking.
He's outside, waiting.
                    They swop places.
                                I watch.
She comes over to me, holds out two fifty pence coins,
Have y'any change – these went straight through.
I swop them for coins in my hand. Hers are cold,
mine are warm. *It's his mam,* she says, *real poorly.*
I rummage in my pockets, find more silver.
Here's three more. I'll use a fiver for my fare.
We smile different smiles.
                    She returns,
                            tugs open the door,
gives him the coins, then waits. And was it tears
on her face or the same rain as on her thin coat,
her hair, her hands?
                    I couldn't tell.
                           The bus arrives,
I get on, pay, sit, see them stood on the pavement
while they talk, hug,
                    walk into un-street-lit shadows
where they'll soon drape jackets over chair backs,
touch them occasionally to see if they're dry.

Food Bank Wednesday and The Great War

In the side-room behind long tables,
vouchers are counted, while on the shelves
coffee jars, shampoos, nappies are checked
before a shout is heard – *no toothpaste left.*
Mugs with dregs of tea are washed, put away
before coats, gloves, are tugged on, the door locked

and a couple, their last customers,
are pointing at lists on a memorial plaque
no-one else notices: The Fallen In The Great War.
We're closing up. You'll have to come with us now,
into the cold – as they're heard slowly reading out
four or five of them, testing the sounds
for naming a child they're expecting.

Commuters and Icarus in the Brexit snowstorm

A poem launched from W.H. Auden's Musee des Beaux Arts

Beyond Seacombe Terminal's high-reaching arch, snow falls
silently, large-flaked, through every streetlight's glare
but it does not concern them
                              though Pieter Bruegel notices
from beneath his broad-brimmed hat how it touches
umbrellas, beanies, hoods above the head-bowed faces
of those who don't look up when a young man flies past,
flaps his slow wings, loses height, reaches the Mersey,
nor hear his wail before he hits the black water
then soundlessly sinks
                              but Pieter Bruegel recognises
the end of this aspiring high-flier matters
because about economics they were never wrong,
those distant offshore investors who told everyone
they should, or would, or could believe in sunlit days
and ignore fears that snow will make wings too heavy
to carry anyone far
                       so Pieter Bruegel watches
those who don't notice as they shuffle in the queue
how the pavement and road now resemble a shroud.
Snowflakes stick to eyelashes, melt, people blink
as they long for the bus to offer them noise and warmth,
away from what they don't know has happened;
from what will make grief rise up in people like them
when they come to know
                              what Pieter Bruegel knows;
when he'll paint what he's seen as if it happened
at mid-day in sunlight and somewhere else.

On your Google Map screen for Brexit Britain

Where the busy A-road dual-carriageway
divides between one side going into town
and the other away from it, there's a street –
two rows of right-angled terraced houses
with a subway on one side to a row of shops
and a bridge on the other where there's a park.
But for residents or visitors walking in or out,
graffiti scrawled on the tunnel and bridge
is bigly banal and extremely English
and all it says is understood.

The opened window

The old man in the flat across the road is mad.
Each day passers-by stare in
as we hear it, Tchaikovsky's 1812,
and he dances – a leap to each cannon blast,
pirouettes in the Marseillaise refrains
until he stands between the curtains and bows.
But today, when we all knew the election was called,
and breakfast TV was all interviews,
there was no noise. No-one glanced in.
So I went outside and saw him
cutting rosettes from coloured crepe
before frisbeeing them through the window –
blue, yellow, then red. But they flopped,
never held themselves together, were trampled over
while he began with the scissors again.
The old man in the flat across the road is mad.

The Everyman Theatre on Budget Day evening

We pass beggars who finger old tin whistles,
to sit, hear new music, watch bright dancers stretch,
pause, twirl, lift, fling each other's lives upwards

until, facing our final applause they untie knots,
release ropes which sway upwards, beyond
a suspension of disbelief into darkness

because we now believe in ourselves as they smile,
still breathless, deeply breathing in our praise –
far deeper than the orchestrated one-sided cheers
below thin microphone cords that lifelessly hung
when the Chancellor had finally sat, sweaty-palmed –

before we stand, leave past those still playing tunes,
feel fresh air on our faces as everyone looks up,
stares up at darkness, no lowering ropes.

Channel Four's rejection letter

Dear... *One-Earring Will? No* – Dear William, (*be polite!*)
This, as usual, is a gave-us-all-a-good-giggle read –
your un-comical clowns, your inverse transvestites –
and like your sonnets, it's all page-turning stuff. But we need
to make the point, and ironically be blunt (if you follow our wit):
long soliloquies are too complex for our viewers' attention
though we recognise, now, you've less ambiguous smut.
Well done. You've worked on previous reasons for rejection
but you need to know those in our management's offices
love innuendo – they'll find adverts for figs. They're sly.
Now, back to your script. There's a few speeches
that characters memorably shout or whisper as asides
which may become book titles, cliches. So, in this play
we'd prefer the actors had plainer things to say.

Between his chapters, Sir Boris Falstaff elbows his way
backstage

where the cast, unscrewing tops from bottled water, stare
as he brandishes his hip-flask in a flabby-fingered hand, sips
then hollers – What ho, all hail, Rialto carousers! Know ye well
I've followed the plot so far – but now I'm intervening. Give me a kilt,
a plastic helmet, high-viz jacket and magic staff, because

I've some absolutely stupendous ideas for incredibly memorable scenes:
tree-planting at Birnam Wood, photo-ops with royalty at Elsinore,
where I'll enter stage right – I'll always appear from the right –
so you can all forget heavy-footed pent-up meters, as I'll ad-lib
and you'll look up at spot-lit me, enthralled at every convolution I utter
for an hour, a stress-free hero who struts the stage, lauding sunlit uplands
that once were blasted heaths on this non-dyspeptic sceptred isle,
my speech reaching the hearts of the numb-bottomed in the gods

before the dark-looking lady appears, a woman with no frailties,
returning from some nunnery to adulate me. I'll propose; we'll kiss,
ride in a gilded river barge, raise goblets of Malmsey, toast tragedies
which, all revels ended, get swept away like yesterday's dust,
for the play's the thing that'll catch me the crown of the king –

its awesome last scene my coronation as King of The World
when you'll kneel round my throne, invite all to repeat the chant,
Long live England, St. George. All hail our Caesar, Boris MacBeth
till the spotlight fades, and curtains close to rapturous applause.

As the new King's Lord Chamberlain imbibed free wine
while sat in his free seat

he saw the clown already explaining to the king and his lover
                                  that the marriage
to his estranged (though not as strange as him) wife (who'd been
                                  in her own tryst)
had been crushed by an overturned carriage – *so you now*
                                need only one divorce.

After an in-front-of-tabs spot-lit mimed wedding, in loud scene
                                  after loud scene
the king's two sons called each other out over fancy dress,
                                  rivalries, privileges,
taking local or foreign wives, until one got banished
                                  before the last act began

where, after a trumpet fanfare, the sovereign sat upstage
                                  as robed nobles processed,
knelt to pledge allegiance before the clown turned, walked downstage
                                  – opened his arms,
asked the audience if they'd swear loyalty instead. Sudden darkness.
                                  Stuttering applause.

Now in a no longer full theatre the Lord Chamberlain sits
                                  on its make-believe throne
as the writer explains, *It's fiction: a made-up king, country, clown.*
                                  So a play can say
everything we all know (dramatic pause) – *or, as with Lear,*
                                  its end might change?

Again, the wine jug's tipped (he'd poured and sipped sack
all through the play)
while he hears how this plot got stirred *like suet, cinnamon, mace,*
in mincemeat pies;
is reminded he's seen plays – tragedies with dysfunctional rulers,
wives, sons, clowns;

with adulteries, sudden deaths, sibling rivalries – but the list
omits drunkenness!
Because, as the night's crowd soberly walks home, talking over
what's been staged,
the jug's empty. Writer and clown watch the man stand, all three
goblets brim full –

their two unseen hands' fingers crossed behind doublet and hose
when the jug falls
as the one with the power to recommend the next day's beheadings
sways,
steadies himself, slurs *All that's left is the toast* (loud belch)
to The King.

This is all I want to say

Chapter 1
Antony at 28, the first night

It was a Friday. And again I was in love. All afternoon,
      I'd not smoked, chewed gum, and now swung my door wide,
kissed your cheek, grinned, took your bag, noticed, but didn't,
      an old tee-shirt's ironed softness, worn-down shoes,
the tightness of the watchstrap you loosened a little,
      blue fingernails, copper earrings, a mole.

On the 433 we each listened as much as talked,
      ate at Mowgli's, drank large glasses of Valpolicella,
watched the calm candle-flame, felt its warmth, didn't notice
      Take That's songs played over our heads
as we recalled being eight, squabbling with hair pulling, then told
      to sit at separate tables at school.

Afterwards, waiting for the bus, we giggled in the drizzle,
      we held wet hands, I knew I had clean towels,
then watched you walk round my living room, pick things up,
      surprising me with an unexpected chuckle
before, as it rained loudly, I discovered in slow motion
      the unhooking of a bra, naked language of hands.

And later as the downpour slowed to a whisper we lay there
      and I was still in love
as we stretched our legs under the duvet, heard the slow way
      we breathed in, breathed out
while hearing an aircraft, its loud sound taking others elsewhere,
      until it faded, was gone.

Chapter 2
Antony at 29, out with his mates for the early-evening
drink they go for on paydays

Look, this is my news. I know I told you –
                              was it last month
when we was all stood here at the bar – I'm back
                              with Lindy again

and somebody probably said, when I went to
                              get in more beers,
Hey, listen to that – Antony 'n Lindy singing Take That
                              as *loud as before.*

I sing on the bus, then over the heads on the escalator,
                              then in the bath
their Greatest Hits – every chorus, falsetto, then bass…

and this time I know what's involved: me washing up
                              (don't laugh)
after every meal, flowers most weekends, sharing the cost
                              of the mattress,

cards so proclaimingly large you need a marker pen
                              to write with,
the quiet joy of identical door-keys, bringing home
                              stories from work

and charming her mum and dad. All to keep her impressed,
                              endlessly.

Chapter 3
The repeating sadness in Antony's 30th year

We watched Groundhog Day on video,
sullen, silent, then slept
snoring like fractured conversation
and this morning I trod on blossom
stuck like confetti on the pavement

after a night of endless rain,
after him across the road
said he found sherry bottles dumped
in their wheelie bin most mornings
on her way to her Tesco's shift

and I felt as if I knew that
although I didn't.

Chapter 4
In Antony's 31st year, what happened

This is all I want to say

Chapter 5
Antony at 40 remembering a decade ago

on a morning when Lindy hardly noticed the sun
rising above the clouds like a gaudy ribbon's knot
as, pregnant, she stood naked by the window
holding flat layers of hair horizontal
while whisking the hairdryer below and above
then brushing it down. I marveled at the silence
undisturbed by the whir till she started to sing
along with Robbie Williams on the radio
then lowered and shook her head, tied her hair –
oh, its gleam in the loosening sun – and her eyes
as she looked at herself in the mirror, smiled
then looked at me, a smile lasting many seconds
that took all these years to reach me, replaying itself
like an old video on the morning's closed curtains.

Chapter 6
Antony at 41 rambling on to a stranger (after a few solitary lunchtime pints) about the dinosaur's egg

We'd come to see the egg,
incubated for ever.

Imagine the size of a dinosaur!
Then Cheryl, peering through glass –
it's a stone.

We'd left the museum for cheeseburgers,
fizzy drinks, ice-cream.

She must be – what – eleven.
Her mother re-married,
There's another child aged eight.

I brood over the fossil,
knowing, now, its weight.

Chapter 7

The epilogue
Cheryl Stone returns to start her first spring term

Her key, pushing into the lock, sounds like her new name, Chez,
before she gets into her yet-to-be-cluttered room to unpack.
She puts files on the desk, squeaks open the empty wardrobe's drawer,
stacks tee-shirts on top of a sipped-from vodka bottle then pushes it shut,
turns on the tap, waits for hot water, sees in the mirror
she's weary, hears squeals of *Great to see you again*
as suitcase-wheels clatter along the corridor's tiles.

Soon, Tom will see her lit window, knock gently,
enter with a smile, expect a kiss and a cuddle then coffee.
While waiting she blutacs selfies to the wall of pint-swigging nights,
and a column down the mirror: topmost, one of her dad in his flat.
Below that, Mum, stepsister, Christmas lunch overcooked; poked-at plates.
When she rubs on eye-shadow each morning they'll grin, motionless,
whisper *Do you still belong with us?* as she slowly blinks.

The journey on her one-glove Friday

In the months of everyone wearing gloves, she'd sit on the same seat,
one by one pinch her gloves' finger-ends, pull hers off slowly.

Now the warm days are here, she holds her clutch-bag tight – gloved hands
snapping it open-and-shut the whole journey, repeating, repeating.

Monday, no mascara. Tuesday, no lipstick. Wednesday, no earrings.
Yesterday her brooch, the floral knotted scarf, went unworn

and today, dishevelments: dangling thread from a lost jacket button,
her blouse's collar half in, half out; un-paired hair slides, a single glove

which she removes, bag snapping open, then tugs off a ring, hesitates,
drops each inside, takes out her phone, then snaps it shut; bare-fingered

types a text. Breathes. Then her naked thumb hits Send
as she speeds past a final cluttered back yard, comes to open fields.

Miss Roberta Frost and the owls

She's so used to being acquainted with nights
when all is black through windows flecked with rain
that gleam like engagement ring trays under lights,
when she gazes beyond them along the lane
of leafless trees, fields emptied of sugar beet,
by the one she wants to come back, explain.

All she hears is the pad of shoes as her feet
climb the stairs to undress, lie still, and the cry
of an owl cruising along his airborne street,
unseen, always aware, not saying good-bye
to his mate but telling her where he is – height
and distance – as he ghosts the empty sky.
Then he answers her call, turns. It's still alright
to hear voices, find where she is in the night.

The tenth of September, two decades on

This night in New Brighton
she'll once again relive the dust,

be overwhelmed by its darkness,
cough, taste its unforgettable bitterness,

remember she'd emptied her shoes,
wiped it from under her watchstrap

then, limp-armed in the shower,
looked down at the stained swirl.

Tomorrow, like each year,
she'll brush unseen grit

from her lowered head,
her now-white hair.

In the hour of the British Summer Time instant

On the hour: torn-up wedding photographs on her carpet
become whole again.

At five past: after his shift a shelf-stacker from Tesco's
places sandwich packs alongside people
asleep in doorways.

At ten past: a coma patient hears not only conversation
but feels a finger squeezed by a baby
she's never seen.

At a quarter past: an old homeless cat dreams again
of a tin-opener's scratch.

At twenty past: two leopards in the zoo wake up,
sense the wind has brought air
that's passed over African savannahs.

At twenty-five past: a bully is scared by frightened eyes staring
up at her and she trembles, yelps and wakes.

At half past   a bruised infant sings his drunken mother
to sleep.

At twenty-five to: the asylum seeker's phone lights up
with a text from his sister
that says she's in Dover.

At twenty to: two married Muslim men with tickets
to Ontario meet and kiss
in a departure lounge.

At a quarter to: a politician weeps, sees on his iPhone
an early edition of The Mail On Sunday:
its front page headline with his name.

At ten to: the teenager slips the knife back into
his pocket.

At five to: a biker feels a touch on his wrist; hears
beyond speeding air a voice
        that calmly says, slow down.

On the hour: an almost-pause ... then everything that's
never happened
may from this instant begin.

This is not about bus travel through the Mersey Tunnel

while I and others are passing through. Neither is it
about the conversation those behind me are having
detailing who said what, where, when, to whom and why
as one I can't see tells of many things said, how they matter,
and the other who listens, repeatedly says I see in the gloom
as she inwardly sees what may or may not be understood.

It's also not about what's above us: the tidal movement of water,
impermeable rock, the faint-blue tunnel-air's haze that hovers,
percolates diesel's stench into our lungs as we pass dim lights
while the bus follows red brake lights until they brightly, suddenly
stop. We, too, stop. This moment an almost pause, like death
which is the big one we'll know but simultaneously won't

because it'll come so we won't know it. But now we trust the bus
will move. It eventually does. We rise, see sunlight which shrives us
and the world we share with each other on its surface begins again
much like it will always begin without us being here. But now
we pass someone in bus-wheel-width, stooped-body-length letters
re-painting SLOW onto tarmac, which we pass ever – so – slowly.

Outside St. George's Hall, Liverpool, midsummer's night

Under tall streetlights when the city's clocks strike twelve
Victoria and Albert, who puts on his top hat, dismount,
watch as forty figures step from their friezes: many naked,
some children, women gathering their drapes
                         so they look more decent when they move
then look back, help others clamber down to gather on the cobbles

where they grin, hug, talk, then hold hands, form a circle
dance lightly in the almost-warm darkness, moving faster, faster,
then, out of breath, stop. Laughter. Some sit on steps,
                              cuddle then kiss
before, in harmony, they sing what they've known for centuries,
gentle songs at first, then the bawdy lyrics that belong to tonight

then many simply stand, stare at the moon, name dimly-lit
                             stars and planets
or point to buildings, floodlit silhouettes that are familiar again
while Victoria and Albert smile, stroll between them. She takes off
                             her jacket,
gives it to a shivering woman. He gives his hat to a bashful man
to cover what his hands try to hide as everyone saunters around

until they hear the clock's chime. They count in unison – again,
                             twelve times.
And on the last stroke become solemn, walk slowly back to the wall,
climb up to where they belong to be gazed at, in sunlight, by those
who'll never know this unsilent hour, their bodies unmoving,
                         their faces again unmoved

How, tonight, a detective sergeant's wife will have her
sadness taken from her

Leaning back, sipping coffee to keep awake,
he's evaluating witness statements, incident reports
of suspected criminal activity, photos of indistinct footprints,
and knows from the chatter of Neighbourhood Officer mates
even pensioners at the bowling club now anxiously believe
something hovered in the aisle in Sainsbury's late that night
behind a widow whose gin bottles chinked in her basket
before she stopped, chuckled, returned each to the shelf

and he lives there, too, so believes witnesses are reliable;
knows in the pub near closing time there's loud whispers
that say more than the cloths of window-cleaners touching windows;
how an invisible creature emerges from the bushes after dusk
before a head leans forward, breathes on the double glazing…
and now, as he's reading, arms slide through the glass
to hug his wife so lightly as, again, she sobs when alone
until, without knowing why, she turns and feels calm.

The effrontery of undercover naming in the C.I.D.

I've claimed the ID of the Copper In Disguise who's thieved my name,
but I still glance at corner seats in pubs in case he's laughing
while he tells lies to impress, persuade those who'll tell secrets
to believe he's as genuine as me. Perhaps he's phoned for the same jalfrezi,
picked it up from the same curry house while I held open the door.
I might have changed his fiver for coins at the car park's machine.
Maybe when I paid in one hundred pounds at the ATM in the bank
he was typing, head down, next to me, taking one hundred out …

But I've read George Herbert said, *Living well is the best revenge.*

So I claim the holiday in Majorca with his wife and family,
play Scrabble with the kids and her parents after Sunday lunch,
put down ENQUIRIES, EXPOSED, each over a triple word square,
and maybe his daughter – my daughter – will look up to me,
yawn, glance back to me at bedtime, sigh *'nite Dad.*
But when he returns to his own home and identity,
pulls open the drawer where he'll find only my socks,
I'll be watching his eyes – an unseen shadow in the dark.

Before becoming Nick Saint in the late afternoon

Gloom looms over the guy who's paused across the street.
Hi Nick, he calls, It is Nick isn't it? You're Nick, Nick Saint.
Head down I walk on, ignore him who thinks I'm not me.
I'm sure, then, I see gloom enter him. It's what I first saw
in exhaust fumes rising through emptied supermarket trolleys
as crammed boots were squeezed shut, as blank faces drove away.

Gloom is in step with my shadow as I reach *Kevin's Kutz*
where a bald barber wearing a Santa beard waves scissors mid-air
while he yells at the queue sat in Santa hats along the wall,
their strangers' faces; and their faces in the salon's facing mirrors
look back at him, at my opening-the-door face: *Everything is gloom*
(which deadens McCartney's Wonderful Christmastime on DVD) –
and the air you'll walk into with fresh necks exposed
will drench you in gloom on tonight's Christmas Eve night out.

I walk on; pause when I only feel it behind the back of my head.
It falls away when Christmas tree lights overwhelm a window
where a couple and child are standing as if they expect someone.

Elsewhere she'll fumble her flat's key into the lock

I'm still looking at a Friend Request, a young woman –
Jaylene Brightway – in a ribbon-adorned US army uniform
on a sunlit porch, a tied-back-tight-ponytail-haloed smile,
and her listed Facebook friends, each with glossy teeth,
shown in a photo squeezed round a table in MacDonald's.
And how many of them are click-my-box trolls, too,
in the same fluorescent-lit fourth floor room in St. Petersburg,
keyboard-clicking demotivational posts on their afternoon shift.
Will she then wait for a tram with a half-full shopping bag
cursing herself quietly because, even though it's pay day
and she's bought her son socks, she forgot a lightbulb.
So, again, she'll walk the corridor to her flat in the dark.

How nae to see ourselves as ithers see us
It wad frae mony a blunder free us,
Tae see oursels as ithers see us
                              Rabbie Burns

Be unrecognizable as the actor
                    who (after his soap opera years
end in a well-publicised death)
                    meets a fellow dog walker –
a club singer who performs under another name,
                    wears a toupee.
Both pull down scarves from faces,
                    ask how things are going
then shiver as they gaze through mist
                    at the slowly rising sun.

Be cool-headed when Facebook recommends Friends
                    you know aren't friendly,
cold-stare when Amazon algorithms appear
                    that suggest more books
because they're so similar to the one you bought
                    from them last week.

Be chilled-out when Netflix texts *You must*
                    change your password
because your account is being used on a TV
                    in Cambridge
while you're visiting family, nibbling popcorn,
                    watching a film.

Believe you're the one who waves
                    at CCTV cameras,
sidles into a side street, returns
                    warmly slouch-shouldered,
head down in a different hat,
                    so is never seen again.

M/s Eyre's lover visits a writers' course at Lumb Bank

He squints up at skylarks, down at the grouse
                        he's disturbed on Widdop Moor,
finds where he'll sit unseen on the wall and
                        hear banter as writers appear,
find benches, nibble slow lunches, laugh
                        as clear as thrushes' songs.

All day, as wine bottles empty he listens,
                        becomes a shadow under the moon
then creeps up creaking stairs, ghosts between rooms,
                        ignores snores,
borrows someone's laptop, sits at the long table,
                        types his name into Google
realises he's still only Jane's lover with passions
                        that drench like storms
or assuage like slow valley mists. That's all.
                        There's no cliffs above heaths
where couples may sit, gaze at fiery clouds
                        that fringe lingering sunsets.

So anger, un-shown by dark-eyed actors, rises;
                        phrases flow down the screen
as, after mingling, hearing the all-day chatter,
                        his fingers flicker,
make paragraphs that describe sentence by sentence
                        his wannabe life,
then, closing the lid, he tiptoes out to where birds sing.

Almost meeting Keats on the doorstep
'So in my veins red life might stream again' John Keats

A pale-faced twenty-something stands outside the villa
leaning on a doorpost, coughs then counts his coins again.
A couple step past him and glance as if they know his face
before one turns to the other, *It's spitting with rain*
but let's hope tonight the stars are bright.

He coughs, smiles politely, asks for one euro so that he can get in.
They ignore him and keep talking – *the bedroom and bed were so tiny.*
Only the wallpaper's changed. Locals were scared of infection.
T.B.'s so contagious. Apart from that, it's the same as when he died.
They keep chatting, open an umbrella in his face. He turns away.

People on the Spanish Steps, walking up or coming down,
step around him, pause, drizzle dripping from wet hair
staring at an upstairs window. He opens a notebook, scribbles,
water dribbling over words. Then he holds it over his mouth.
Coughs. Coughs again. Blood flecks the cover once more.

I'm with you, MacNeice, in your living room

and while you scrawl, all's suddenly rich with Bushmill's colour
as its gleam radiates above doilies that imitate shapes snowflakes have
before they splay, stick, liquify on panes after their ceaseless fall
onto a world that's crazier than you or I, that is tipping itself out
like this emptying bottle between us, as we squat between plates of
tangerine peel as we know the randomness of sudden

drunken
thoughts.

We watch the fire's blaze caught in globules that were once snow
which run down the window like supposed disasters. We pour,
lift topped-up glasses, look through them. Truths rise like sparks
when a rose-patterned log falls onto another in the grate

and their plurality reassures us that the warmth we're feeling
is not just from what's burning or from whiskey, but belongs
in a world where snow's soundless melting moves beyond
more than glass, more than us, more and much further.

Hi Wystan,

Please excuse me being so familiar.
Although we both loved Alston, that's not enough
to feel we share anything that's similar
except a love of poems and dislike of duff
rhymes. I still wonder, did your smokers' cough
interrupt rhythms, scatter spittle on scansions?
As you worked in slippers for clearest meanings

before you walked, sodden feet squelching in puddles
that mottled Housesteads' car-park with swathes of rain
as you were taken to visit Hadrian's Wall
to be driven back, clothes soaked, chain-smoking
another packet of Senior Service, sullen.
So I thought I'd type an email to you
saying I've heard of your own Roman Wall Blues.

But I also recall other poets who met
as they travelled, like Shelley in Italy
who, though well scared, met Byron and yet
while the rain siled down, the Lord challenged Percy
to write and when lightning flared, Mary –
while the lads drunkenly snored – by candle-flame
began scrawling Frankenstein. It made her name

like Don Juan made his. But he hated the north –
Seaham, with a wife, was not his great good place.
He became more mad, bad, dangerous to know, moved south.
On a map in your shack on Fire Island you'd trace
with a nicotined finger your homesickness
for the land, but you felt unease with those who're moved
by what you wrote about the region they love.

And you wrote to Byron who didn't reply –
you can't either – from wet Reykjavik, revealing
some life stories, much wit, thoughts on poetry
and, like your mate MacNeice, we smiled as you sang
exciting simple rhymes with sounds as striking
as a match's sharp rasp; but your poet's talk
was to yourself – in English not Icelandic –

which is what poetry can sometimes be called
when someone's almost listening at your elbow
who nods in agreement because our memories hold
similar thoughts to the fiery Lord and you,
but we never light up language as well, though
I'm trying to put in this e-mail that I get it:
feel a wet-slipper slouch, Byron's shin-kicking club foot.

LOL,

Bob

So unlike Maya Angelou

I live with a canary.
        It circles me,
                twitters, while talons pinch my shoulder;
interrupts thoughts like a phone
        before I pick up a pen.

                I feed it. It knows that.
But I know its glare, how its claws scratch,
        feathers ruffle, when I prod
                its delicate body into the cage

before I drape the plain cloth over its frame
        then sit in everywhere's loud silence
                listening, listening.

If you discover you're in a Bob Cooper poem

you'll be the first, second, or a third person,
loitering or sitting, watching what others do
and you'll hear me chatter, ask a question
before your quick answer astonishes you.
There may be others you don't expect,
like film extras, and you stand with them.
You may not matter. But you may.

It might be night, or at any time of day
when you'll notice something ordinary
that gleams with extraordinary significance
and see things that aren't mentioned, too.
Don't be afraid to touch things or leave them be.
Changes may have happened before the poem began
or could happen later. You'll realise that.
Just feel welcome. Be there. And wonder

whether to expect an explosion – maybe an IED,
because there's an attentive phone in a dark bag
crammed with images, suggestions to startle
as they fling out memories, ignite realisations,
and, as you read this, is there one in your hand,
and is either of you holding your breath.

O'Hara and Melly meet up in Liverpool

In the News From Nowhere Bookshop Frank's signing books,
What's your name? Carol Ann. OK. when George shows up,
                                                bold as his suit,
a lily and ferns drooping from his buttonhole, a multi-floral silk shirt,
and a squidged-full Asda bag,
                    I've just been in Oxfam, got new old clothes,
there's someone homeless called Dave two doorways down from here.
I'll give him this bag. Quality tat I bought in Jermain Street.
                                Frank smiles, chooses a book,
Paul Reverdy's Selected, pays cash from the pocket over his heart.

So they chat to the cruise-ship chef who lives below window menus,
hear a saxophonist, see a gold-laméd Billie Holliday beside him.
                                                They stop,
drop rummaged-for coins into his case, hear them tinkle like cymbals
as Billie looks at their faces, sings softly, knowingly, into their eyes,
Lover Man – and all street noises pause – *(Oh, Where Can You Be?)*

as George says more about Egyptian Surrealism, the new Exhibition,
You ain't seen nothing like it where you're from.
                                The Green Man flashes,
they cross, pressed close in the crowd.
                                Frank pauses, says *Lunch?*
gets two hotdogs, George buys 99s. They slow-chew, slowly lick,
before
        – and this they rarely do –
                                they tell of their sailor-boy lives.
George loved bell-bottom trousers; Frank, tee-shirts' tight fit.

And on they walk –
                George's hair and lily flopping; Frank's hair-loss
hidden by a baseball cap with New York and a neon heart –
                            and talk,
share familiar words, not-quite-hidden meanings, until they're there:
their backs to Albert Dock's squared water, in before they open
                  see-yourselves-together glass doors of The Tate

where George no longer sees colours, backdrops to lusty blues,
Frank doesn't hear cool jazz only heard in New York,
                        instead
they walk slower, stop as shapes of a new music drift closer,
                          touch.

Constantine Cavafy and the Galatasaray Penalty

As drizzle falls, drunks in identical glossy red shirts
link arms as if under a lover's moon, lift their heads,
sashay across the road, and with smooth soft accents
croon incantations of players' names.
                                    He avoids eye-contact,
writes in his notebook, *Love flows from drainpipe to puddle
like sex* ... then crosses it out.
                                    Always on the pavement,
he's come out, a yearning eighteen year-old writing poems
of desire for football supporters, moist clothes outlining bodies
as they cram into the over-full pub to watch the match
in the Turk Telekom Stadium. The European Cup: Liverpool
versus the Champions, Galatasaray.
                                    His breath's held –
there, beside the floodlit pitch, in the exultant crowd's faces –
as he stands at a window, peers through condensation
and watches, above heads, the big screen
                                    shares the silence
as slo-mo close-ups from different angles are repeated
before he sees a striking player. His stare. The ball on the spot.
Its gleam. Then hears the TV's distant roar, local groans. A goal.
And he scribbles again, before – two-handed – lifting his book
to sway it slow and wide like a scarf, sing with wet eyes and lips:

> *Ω φωτισμένος Θεός της Κωνσταντινούπολης
> Είμαι χορτασμένος από πολλές αγάπες.
> Πέτα μου τη φανέλα σου, Ω υπέροχο σκόρερ.
> Ας παίξουμε ως ντόπιοι βάρβαροι.*

Like Philip Larkin and the cold content of pies

Maybe there's still someone like Larkin
who puts down a pork pie on a plate, pours gin, tonic,
deftly pulls vinyl from its sleeve, blows it for dust,
watches the arm swing, slowly lower so that the quiet hiss
that introduces Bechet begins, before he sits

and, like Larkin, listens, relaxes, nibbles, remembers
the gristle in a half-eaten one on a Sheffield station platform.
The buffet was closing so he'd stood, starved, in the wind,
melancholically seeing a full moon as an ironic unbitten pie.

He snaffles a bite. Pastry crumbs smatter his trousers
like confetti Larkin saw scattered, when in a London train,
over some who'd got on, sat, squirmed, giggled, sighed
as the train pulled away, while he scribbled in a notebook.
But here, nothing's brushed off; not even to jazz. Fingers lie flat

unlike Bechet's melodies, so finger-deft; raunchy as pies
shared in bed, stripped to their vests like Larkin and Monica
when they ate what they'd bought in the village on a Show Saturday
and hands briefly felt warmth they'd forgotten they knew

and now, beyond Larkin's writing, he's more than half-drunk
before Bechet's breathed-out jazz floats over his snores
until the hiss-click repetition after the LP's last track;
the see-through glass, dull bottle, plate all empty on the carpet
when he uncoils, yawns, takes it all in, shuffles upstairs.

Huge Ted's last morning

Say it anyway you want, he was abundantly private,
even as a kid in the tobacconists in Mexborough
or re-walking through leaves above Mytholmroyd.
Whatever else he did he's still the night-watchman,
the beekeeper, the rose-gardener they'd known; a farmer
whose now thin fingers you can hardly believe
yanked out a dead lamb; whose ears still seem to hear
footballers in the Pennine rain, their violent words.
And the last salmon he caught's still in the fridge,
its oil and pink weight collapsing in on itself
until all that remains is the language he gave us,
the books we'll re-open, and the deep-vowelled
fuck, said with the nakedness of an old man
lifted from the bath for the last time.

After taking Seamus Heaney to Wetherspoons in West Kirby

I imagine his head-back laugh when he'll sit all night
telling unlikely likeable stories from the Other Country
then with a grin full as a tray of beer glasses
he'll high-five everyone before we'll leave, stand in crisp air –
breath and joy rising in clouds beneath streetlights –

before he'll pause, pick up a lily from the gutter,
gently stroke it, rummage in many pockets,
pull out a crumpled till-receipt, ask for a pen,
stand in the road, frown, smile, scrawl a line,
but the last train would be in, so we'll rush –

board it, breathless, and sit, legs stretched,
then he'll lower his head, his chest rising, falling
as he mumbles sleep-words; as the train sways
while his dreams stagger with the drunkenness of things.

At the sixth station he'll wake, stare at the dark,
collect his thoughts. *Everywhere here was bog,* I'll say.
What's half-submerged rises into poems, he'll mumble
then smile, scribble a phrase before he'll slumber again.
I'll watch the flower, my pen in his jacket top pocket,
until we're under the Mersey where the tunnel's roar
will startle him. *Is that Grendel's mother?* he'll yell
before the carriages slope up on the Liverpool side.

I'll lead him, drowsy, not yet sober, up to the street
where we'll stroll past midnight shops to his hotel.
There, we'll shake hands. He'll thank me.
Mighty fine craic, we'll agree. I'll ask for my pen
then watch him walk through the glass door,
wave, before the lift takes him upwards
to re-enter his long silent dark room
to sleep fully clothed, the lily on his chest.

Tonight's Free Event: Yevgeny Yevtushenko in Waterstones

In a knitted jacket, vivid shirt, he gazes around,
So many, so much poetry books. Ah, in America,
nowhere, nothing like this. His accent strong.
Then football – a Red Army striker who quoted Pasternak,
politics, stood with Yeltsin outside the Kremlin on a tank.
Wives (no number, no comment), literature, *Poosh-kin's*
pages and pages of poetry – and then he begins.

We hear stanzas that still cycle round Moscow in sunlight,
talk like uncles at Zima Junction; hear elegies sing
from Kyiv's silent earth at Babir Yar. But he's autumn now,
no longer precocious spring. Yet he takes his hands from pockets
of Russian charm, American brag, to dive at our feet
with a goal-keeper's verve; a table-tennis player's wrist
loops words in the air. We applaud. *Spasibo, oh thank you.*

Yes, I've written 720,000 lines, thirty percent of them good.
On Thursday another novel I complete. He walks past us,
eyes bright as his clothes, sits, overwhelms both table, chair,
signs books that can't touch untranslatable loss. M*y name*
is Ukrainian. It was my mother's. Russians wanted freedom -
now they queue outside McDonald's. Putin stares like Stalin.
He shakes our hands, says all this, before – *no more poems.*

W. S. Graham and Nessie Dunsmuir at Meols: the never-written holiday poems

1. They listen while they're putting on lunch

Sydney's jotted phrases on Post-it Notes
are now stuck on the caravan's cupboard doors.
Each time he stops, looks, he discovers
they say far more than their words.
Sometimes he looks beyond them,
stares at shelves, picks out what's there,
reads small-print ingredient lists,
instructions and timings on packets

but right now

stood between his idioms and him
Nessie makes lunch. Grips the crust
as the knife saws into a three-day-old bloomer
then spreads Flora from an almost empty tub,
lays a thin slice of tongue, then the top slice,
lifts it like a couplet to bite into slowly
while Sydney's laptop boots itself up
as he sits, tight-lipped; as a gull is heard
walking the roof like finger-clicks on a keyboard
while he waits and she wordlessly chews

then he stares at the screen,
watches the YouTube video again –
a glacier that belongs in another land –
begins to discover what emerges
when the poem on his split-screen began
to show its lines as creaking breaks in ice
where he now sees what crevasses reveal
as his writing's slow weight shifts

but then he pauses

lifts his head at the local gull's squeal –
a call announcing to the air there's food –
while his newly-typed words try to imitate,
glide, circle, wheel, swoop, take
what the bird's language is using them for

as the glacier calves an iceberg
which noiselessly sways away,
becomes a plain surface stanza,
it's depth invisible to a gull's eye
as it uses language's silences
to hide, hint at, much more.

2. The nightfishermen's gift

He phones, apologises for being so late
but he's ended up at Perch Rock –
and I'm still talking with these fishermen.

Which fishermen?
                    Those I met in the pub.
But Nessie doesn't ask which pub –
an explanation would waste the battery.
Instead she says, *It's dark. I'm hungry.*
Have you bought food? But he's not listening.
Instead he's talking, *Whist, woman. Peel potatoes,*
open the tin of mushy peas. I've got cod.

Bending over the table he pulls out
the biggest fish they'd caught that night
which they gave him, slithered into a Tesco bag,
and with the sharpest knife the caravan has,
he stares at its dark eye, severs beyond the gill,
lays its gut aside to throw out for the gulls,
unpeels its spine's comb from flesh; remembers,
as it bent, flicked, died, someone called his name:
Sydney, quick! Look at it – so the last thing it sees
is the face of the one who'll stomach it.
Now, sobering up as the cooker's gas hisses,
potatoes boil, the grilled gutted fish curls,
he says, *do fish dream, in their living depths?*
After supper, I fear dark dreams will talk.

3. Before the five English lessons

Through another caravan's open door Sydney sees
the quietness of flute-assembling –
how the cork lining surrounding the crown's end
is sucked, squeezed with a wiggle into the female hole
then twisted before the third part's pushed in, aligned.
Levers are then lifted as felt tabs are examined
until fingertips hold its hollow blackness,
raise it to the horizontal, where he pauses, lips pursed,
and blows, gently, smoothly, so breath flows
invisibly from mouth to spread around audible air.
Now, wordless sound becomes more than a tune
as it unquietly dips, rises (so like a gull's flight),
soothes, before he realises he's being watched.
They look at each other, smile.

Walking from bus-stop to their caravans,
breath rises in the twilight, merges in the cold
as he mentions the flute he carries is *my Grandad's.*
I brought it with safeness from Helmand.
We have six berths. Housing people okay the rent.
I live with seven others. I floor-sleep not well.
Each day I play on steps at Lime Street Station.
People give small coins but I never can smile
or speak. Today a family waiting for train
stand five songs with me. I get no clapping.
They took with them my music, but to where?
He pauses.

       My English speaking is nothing good.
Will you teach me improvement?

                       Sydney grins,
remembers how it was all pieced together
and how, from constructed space, he heard it
articulate air. And now, while gulls sleep,

distant owls communicate, says *Aye, let's do that.*
You'll learn me how to learn how words sing, too,
coz you're an artist with sound, and so is your language
that's also open from your almost closed flautist's lips.
I'll gift you my accent, grammar's harmonies, phrases.

*4. After finding the car keys in the just-packed suitcase
Nessie speaks the final not-written holiday poem*

*Sydney – take my hand,
turn your back*

*on this lengthening sand, shrinking sea,
as gliding gulls wheel, squeal cries*

*to language's silence
before poems' phrases are born.*

*Did you forget to wind your watch?
Our time here's complete.*

*Come, let us journey
this driving day,*

*open-windowed
on the word-road home.*

NAKEDEYEPUBLISHING.CO.UK

Notes

Mr Yeats's radio recording of when he and Mr Pound spent a February afternoon in Hoylake

Ezra Pound, in the ABC Of Reading, claimed that he knows a lot about Beethoven yet Yeats didn't know the difference between a G and a B#. So, is Yeats having a dig at his once friend by saying he likes Rod Stewart's singing?

A retired shipyard draughtsman hears the ghost-pilot's song

The Three Graces are the Royal Liver Building, the Cunard Building, and the Port of Liverpool Building on the Pier Head.

Pensioners remember Wilson Pickett

Wilson Pickett's *In The Midnight Hour* was in the UK charts in September 1965.

Commuters and Icarus in the Brexit snowstorm

Pieter Bruegel painted 'Landscape with the Fall of Icarus' in 1588. The original is lost but a copy hangs in the Musée des Beaux-Arts, Brussels. The Seacombe Ferry Terminal is near New Brighton. It's also okay if you hear W. H. Auden's typewriter faintly clicking behind the poem.

Ob-La-Di, Ob-La-Da was a number one hit for Marmalade in January 1969

As the new King's Lord Chamberlain imbibed free wine while sat in his free seat

In a theatre the tabs are the curtains that are occasionally draped between the full stage and the audience. Incidental scenes are sometimes acted in front of the tabs. In Shakespeare's The Merry Wives Of Windsor, Falstaff says: "Go fetch me a quart of sack; put a toast in't" – the toasted bread being intended to make the wine more drinkable. Oh, and belching in public wasn't acceptable. A few years later Samuel Pepys wrote: "Men of the early seventeenth century were models of courtesy and good manners..." Maybe this incident gave Shakespeare the idea of calling one of his characters Sir Toby Belch.

M/s Eyre's lover visits a writers' course at Lumb Bank

Lumb Bank is an Arvon Writing Centre just below the top edge of Heptonstall. A walk from Top Withens, the fictional Wuthering Heights, is a pleasant summer's walk via Widdop's moorlands.

The effrontery of undercover naming in the C.I.D.

The quotation is from proverb number 524 in 'Outlandish Proverbs' selected by George Herbert and printed by T. Paine for Humphrey Blunden at The Castle in Corn-hill, London, 1640.

Almost meeting Keats on the doorstep

The quotation 'So in my veins red life might stream again' is from a small, untitled momento mori poem that begins, 'This living hand, now warm and capable', by John Keats (1819).

One of the times when Willie Long-Legs and Laudanum Sam met Mazy Mary and Sarah Snuggles

The Hutchinson sisters, Mary and Sarah, lived in Sockburn Hall. Peg Powler is a river nymph that enticed and drowned men in the River Tees. The Sockburn Worm was a local monster... but any link either to the Jabberwock and Coleridge's state of mind after too much laudanum is coincidental.

Constantine Cavafy and the Galatasaray penalty

Cavafy attended school in Liverpool. When much older he visited Istanbul, which was previously called Constantinople. Galatasaray is one of Istanbul's football teams.

This non-surviving fragment of Cavafy's juvenilia can be transcribed as:

O floodlit God of Constantinople
I'm saturated with many loves.
Throw me your shirt, O gorgeous scorer.
Let us play as local barbarians.

In later life it was noticed he read his poems in Greek but with a Liverpool accent.

Naked Eye Publishing

A fresh approach

Naked Eye Publishing is an independent, not-for-profit micro-press intent on publishing quality poetry and literature.

A particular focus is literature in translation. We aim to take a midwife role in facilitating the translation of works that have until now been disregarded by English-language publishing. We will be happy if we function purely as an initial stepping-stone both for overlooked writers and first-time literary translators.

Each of us at Naked Eye is a volunteer, competent and professional in our work practice, and not intending to make a profit for the press. We see ourselves as part of a revolution in book publishing, embodying the newly levelled playing field, sidestepping the publishing establishment to produce beautiful books at an affordable price with writers gaining maximum benefit from sales.

nakedeyepublishing.co.uk